I0799585

STUDY GUIDE

Sojourners and Exiles

The Message of First Peter

Sinclair B. Ferguson

Ligonier Ministries
Renew your Mind.
LIGONIER.ORG | 800-435-4343

421 Ligonier Court, Sanford, FL 32771
Email: info@ligonier.org

Printed in China.

Contents

Introduction 3

Study Schedules 5

1 *A Tract for Our Times* 6

2 *Glory in Our Grief* 13

3 *Do We Belong Here?* 20

4 *A Love the World Wants* 27

5 *The Royal Family* 34

6 *Living in Two Worlds* 41

7 *Returning to Eden* 48

8 *Blessing Our Enemies* 55

9 *Arm Yourselves* 62

10 *How Should Christians Suffer?* 69

11 *Shepherds Who Show the Way* 76

12 *Bound for Glory* 83

Introduction

In recent years, many Christians have felt more and more like strangers in a hostile culture. The Apostle Peter wrote a letter to a church living in a similar situation. First Peter teaches us that the gospel empowers Christians to live faithfully anywhere and at any time. In *Sojourners and Exiles,* Sinclair Ferguson shows us what great encouragement we can find in this letter written to Christians going through a "fiery trial" in a pagan empire.

This study guide is a companion to the video teaching series. Whether you are using the DVDs, streaming the videos on Ligonier.org, or going through the course in Ligonier Connect, this resource is designed to help you make the most of the learning experience. For each message in the series, there is a corresponding lesson in this guide. Here is what you will find in each lesson:

INTRODUCTION	The introduction is a brief paragraph that summarizes the content covered in the lecture and considered in the study guide lesson. **How to use:** Use the introduction to each lesson to get a sense of the big picture before watching the video. Refer to these statements as you work through the study guide to remind yourself of what you have already covered and where you are headed.
LEARNING GOALS	The learning goals are the knowledge and skills that the study guide lesson will endeavor to equip you with as you work through the lecture content. **How to use:** Familiarize yourself with the goals of each lesson before engaging its contents. Keeping the overall purpose in mind as you watch each video and reflect on or discuss the questions will help you get the most out of each lesson.
KEY IDEAS	The key ideas are the major points or takeaways from the lecture. **How to use:** Use these ideas to prepare yourself for each lesson and to review previous lessons. They describe specifically the knowledge that each lecture is communicating.

REFLECTION & DISCUSSION QUESTIONS	The questions are the guided reflection and/or discussion component of the lesson that is intended to help you prepare for, process, and organize what you are learning. **How to use:** Reflect on individually or discuss in a group the questions in the order in which they appear in the lesson. The time stamps in the right margin indicate where the answers to questions during the video can be found.
PRAYER	The prayer section offers suggestions for how to close the lesson in prayer with respect to what was taught in the lecture. **How to use:** Consider using each lesson's prayer section as a guide to personal or group prayer. These sections follow the ACTS prayer model, which you can learn more about in R.C. Sproul's Crucial Questions booklet *Does Prayer Change Things?* This helpful guide is available as a free e-book at Ligonier.org.
REVIEW QUIZ	The review quiz is a set of six multiple-choice questions that appears at the end of each lesson. **How to use:** Use each quiz to check your comprehension and memory of the major points covered in each lecture. It will be most beneficial to your learning if you take a lesson's quiz either sometime between lessons or just before you begin the next lesson in the study guide.
ANSWER KEY	The answer key provides explanations for the reflection and discussion questions and answers to the multiple-choice questions in the review quiz. **How to use:** Use the answer key to check your own answers or when you do not know the answer. Note: Do not give in too quickly; struggling for a few moments to recall an answer reinforces it in your mind.

Study Schedules

The following table suggests four plans for working through the *Sojourners and Exiles* video teaching series and this companion study guide. Whether you are going through this series on your own or with a group, these schedules should help you plan your study path.

	Extended 14-Week Plan	Standard 12-Week Plan	Abbreviated 6-Week Plan	Intensive 4-Week Plan
Week	**Lesson**			
1	*	1	1 & 2	1–3
2	1	2	3 & 4	4–6
3	2	3	5 & 6	7–9
4	3	4	7 & 8	10–12
5	4	5	9 & 10	
6	5	6	11 & 12	
7	6	7		
8	7	8		
9	8	9		
10	9	10		
11	10	11		
12	11	12		
13	12			
14	*			

* For these weeks, rather than completing lessons, spend your time discussing and praying about your learning goals for the study (the first week) and the most valuable takeaways from the study (the last week).

1

A Tract for Our Times

INTRODUCTION

The Apostle Peter wrote his letter to teach Christians how to live in a pagan culture. He offers his original readers comfort by showing how the gospel works even in the hostile Roman society. In this lesson, Dr. Ferguson introduces 1 Peter as a tract for our times. Christians today often feel like cultural outsiders and need to know that the gospel works everywhere and in any age.

LEARNING GOALS

When you have finished this lesson, you should be able to:

- Explain why Christians today should study 1 Peter
- Understand why the Apostle Peter is well suited to offer comfort to suffering Christians
- Describe the Christians who first read this letter

KEY IDEAS

- The gospel works in any culture because Christ is always with His people.
- Peter writes as one who knows from experience what these churches are suffering.
- Christians are those who have been chosen and set apart by God.

REFLECTION & DISCUSSION QUESTIONS

Before the Video

What Do You Think?

Take a moment to answer the following questions. They will prepare you for the lecture.

- Do you ever feel that your faith in Christ makes you a cultural outsider? Why or why not?

- Why do you think God allows His people to suffer?

Scripture Reading

About that time Herod the king laid violent hands on some who belonged to the church. He killed James the brother of John with the sword, and when he saw that it pleased the Jews, he proceeded to arrest Peter also. This was during the days of Unleavened Bread. And when he had seized him, he put him in prison, delivering him over to four squads of soldiers to guard him, intending after the Passover to bring him out to the people. So Peter was kept in prison, but earnest prayer for him was made to God by the church.

—Acts 12:1–5

- What did Peter and the other Apostles experience as described in this passage? How did the church respond? How might knowledge of this event affect the way you read 1 Peter?

During the Video

Answer the following questions while you watch the video. They will guide you through the lecture.

Why Study 1 Peter? *0:00–12:10*

- Why do Christians often find it easy to identify with the Apostle Peter?
- What is the "general reason" that we should study 1 Peter?
- What three attitudes can Christians have when living in an anti-Christian culture?

The Apostle and His Readers *12:10–23:17*

- Why did Peter not complain about the suffering that he and these churches were enduring?
- What are two ways that Peter describes his original readers?

After the Video

Answer the following questions after you have finished the lecture. They will help you identify and summarize the major points.

- Why is 1 Peter a tract for our times?

  If you are in a group, have the members discuss how they tend to imagine the New Testament church. Ask: How is the political and cultural situation of the early church different from that of modern Western culture and how is it similar? How hard is it to relate to the experiences of the first Christians?

- How does the way that Peter identifies himself help us understand the purpose of this letter, and how should we respond to it?

  If you are in a group, have the members discuss what impressions they have of Peter as they begin this study. Ask: How is he like and unlike other Apostles who wrote the New Testament? How easy is it to trust his teaching?

- The Christians who read this letter were chosen and sanctified, or set apart. Who chose them and set them apart? For what purpose were they chosen and set apart?

  If you are in a group, have the members discuss what they think uniquely identifies Christians. Ask: Which aspects of your Christian identity most encourage you? How comforting do you find the identity that Peter applies to these suffering churches?

PRAYER

Commit what you have learned from God's Word in this lesson to prayer.

- Praise God for choosing us to belong to His Son.
- Confess any doubts you have that Jesus is enough for you as you face difficult circumstances.
- Thank God for comforting His people through the promise of Christ's presence.
- Ask God for a growing faith in His providence and promises as you face fear and pain.

REVIEW QUIZ

Use these multiple-choice questions to measure what you learned from this lesson.

1. What makes it easy for many people to identify with the Apostle Peter?
    a. His strong faith
    b. His love of Christ
    c. His failures
    d. His doctrinal clarity
2. Contemporary Western culture is a threat unlike any other that the church has ever faced.
    a. True
    b. False
3. Which of the following is *not* a way that Peter identifies himself in this letter?
    a. Fellow elder
    b. Friend
    c. Eyewitness
    d. Fellow sufferer
4. Thinking about what future experience can help us see our present suffering as light and momentary?
    a. Spiritual growth
    b. Relief from pain
    c. Peace
    d. Glory
5. Which member of the Trinity is mentioned in 1 Peter 1:1–2?
    a. The Father
    b. The Son
    c. The Holy Spirit
    d. All three members of the Trinity
6. What is *not* one of the ways that we as Christians persevere through trials?
    a. Focusing on Christ
    b. Living by the Spirit
    c. Pure positive thinking
    d. Remembering that the Father chose us

Answer Key—A Tract for Our Times

REFLECTION & DISCUSSION QUESTIONS

Before the Video

What Do You Think?

These are personal questions. The answers should be based on your own knowledge and experience.

Scripture Reading

- What did Peter and the other Apostles experience as described in this passage? How did the church respond? How might knowledge of this event affect the way you read 1 Peter?

  The Apostles were persecuted by a political leader, King Herod. James was killed, and Peter was sent to prison. Herod did this to please the church's enemies. The people of the church responded by praying; they called out to God for help. Knowing that Peter faced hostility and persecution can help readers trust his teaching. He has endured trials like those that his readers face.

During the Video

Why Study 1 Peter?

- Why do Christians often find it easy to identify with the Apostle Peter?

  It is easy to identify with Peter because Scripture has recorded his many faults. Peter betrayed Jesus during His earthly ministry. He also wavered as a leader of the early church and was confronted by the Apostle Paul (see Gal. 2:11–14). We often find it easiest to open our hearts to a writer or teacher who shares our weaknesses.

- What is the "general reason" that we should study 1 Peter?

  We should study 1 Peter for the general reason that it is the Word of God. All of the Bible teaches us about the Lord Jesus Christ and how to serve Him. The Scriptures correct us and then heal us spiritually.

- What three attitudes can Christians have when living in an anti-Christian culture?

  First, we can put our heads in the sand and try to ignore potential dangers. Second, we can complain about everything that is going wrong in society. Third, we can find exhilaration in the New Testament's teaching and its relevance to our times.

The Apostle and His Readers

- Why did Peter not complain about the suffering that he and these churches were enduring?

  Peter did not complain about their circumstances because his focus was not on earthly life. His focus was the glory that God will reveal in His people when Christ returns—a glory that Christians begin to experience now. Peter lived his life backward from the future, so even terrible suffering seemed light and temporary.

- What are two ways that Peter describes his original readers?

  Peter describes his readers in terms of their geographical locations and their spiritual identity. Geographically, they were scattered around Asia Minor, the area that is the nation of Turkey today. Spiritually, they were chosen by God and set apart from the world as servants of Christ.

After the Video

- Why is 1 Peter a tract for our times?

  Peter wrote this letter to ancient churches, but their situation is similar to ours. The New Testament church lived centuries before the beginning of "Christendom," the attempt to make whole societies Christian. Peter wrote to churches that faced hostility from a pagan culture, and modern Christians increasingly face hostility as Christian influence on Western society fades away.

- How does the way that Peter identifies himself help us understand the purpose of this letter, and how should we respond to it?

  Peter identifies himself as an Apostle—a "sent one." As an Apostle, he was a witness to Christ and His sufferings and was sent to tell the world about Jesus. Because he is an Apostle, he has authority: readers can know that what he says is true. He also identifies himself as one who has suffered as his readers have. He is not above them. He shows readers that he and they together have fellowship with Christ in their trials.

- The Christians who read this letter were chosen and sanctified, or set apart. Who chose them and set them apart? For what purpose were they chosen and set apart?

  God chose and set apart—sanctified—these Christians. Each person of the Trinity plays a role in this. God the Father chooses Christians before the foundation of the world. He chooses them so that they will be obedient to Christ, God the Son. God the Holy Spirit sets apart or sanctifies those whom the Father has chosen. These things form the identity of Christians.

REVIEW QUIZ

1. **C.**
   While Peter had strong faith and taught sound doctrine and certainly loved our Savior, he can seem easier to identify with than many others in Scripture because his failures are plainly retold through Scripture.

2. **B.**
   Certain aspects of modern culture are new, but living as Christians in a non-Christian society is not new. This was the condition of all Christians for the first three hundred years of the church.

3. **B.**
   Peter identifies himself as an Apostle, an eyewitness of Christ's suffering, a fellow elder, and a fellow sufferer. He does not identify himself as a friend, though his affection for the church is apparent throughout his letter.

4. **D.**
   Christians have peace with God now through the gospel, but Peter emphasizes here the glory that will be revealed in them when Christ returns (1 Peter 1:7). Thinking about this future glory, which in some ways Christians already have, puts our suffering in perspective.

5. **D.**
   Peter mentions all three members of the Trinity in these opening verses. The Father knew us and chose us before He created the world. The Holy Spirit sanctified us or set us apart for God's purposes. Jesus Christ, as our King, saved us through His blood so that we could worship and obey Him.

6. **C.**
   The work of each member of the Trinity contributes to our encouragement and comfort. As we focus on Christ, our Savior and King, live by the power of the Spirit, who does the work of sanctifying us, and remember that the Father has chosen us as His own, we grow in hope and the ability to press on. In a general sense, these truths are "positive," but Peter does not want Christians to focus on whatever makes them feel good and ignore harsh realities. Instead, he wants them to focus on God so that they can persevere and know that their suffering has a purpose.

2

Glory in Our Grief

INTRODUCTION

The Apostle Peter begins his letter by focusing on the gospel rather than the pain of the Christians to whom he is writing. He does this because the gospel is glorious, and only this glory can bring true and lasting comfort. In this lesson, Dr. Ferguson shows how God uses our suffering to make us like Christ and how He reveals His glory in our grief.

LEARNING GOALS

When you have finished this lesson, you should be able to:

- Understand why the gospel is glorious and why this glory comforts Christians
- Explain the purpose of Christian suffering

KEY IDEAS

- Christ's resurrection comforts us by reminding us of our new birth and our future resurrection.
- In His providence, God allows His people to suffer so that they become like Christ.
- Focusing on Christ's suffering and death for us reveals the glory in our own suffering.

REFLECTION & DISCUSSION QUESTIONS

Before the Video

What Do You Think?

Take a moment to answer the following questions. They will prepare you for the lecture.

- When someone tells you about their suffering, how do you tend to respond? What words do you tend to use? When you're suffering, what do you want to hear from others?

- What do you believe the Bible says to those who are suffering? How does it offer comfort? What verses or biblical events come to mind?

Scripture Reading

Blessed be the God and Father of our Lord Jesus Christ, the Father of mercies and God of all comfort, who comforts us in all our afflictions, so that we may be able to comfort those who are in any affliction, with the comfort with which we ourselves are comforted by God. For as we share abundantly in Christ's sufferings, so through Christ we share abundantly in comfort too.

—2 Corinthians 1:3–5

- How is God identified by the Apostle Paul in this passage? What does God do for us when we suffer? Why does He do this?

During the Video

Answer the following questions while you watch the video. They will guide you through the lecture.

What Comforts the Christian? *0:00–12:32*

- How does Satan want Christians to interpret their suffering?

- What comforting words did Jesus speak in John 17?

The Purpose of Christian Suffering *12:32–23:52*

- What is the purpose of trials in the Christian life?

- What blessings does God want us to experience even while we suffer?

- Aside from Christians, who else sees the glory of the gospel?

After the Video

Answer the following questions after you have finished the lecture. They will help you identify and summarize the major points.

- How does Peter comfort these Christians? How is this like or unlike other common ways of offering comfort?

  If you are in a group, have the members discuss what comforts them when they are suffering. Ask: How do you respond to the kind of comfort that 1 Peter offers?

- What is the inheritance of Christians? Why does Peter say that it is glorious?

  If you are in a group, ask the members whether they think often about the resurrection. Ask: If so, do you think of it as a glorious inheritance? How has knowledge of the resurrection helped you face difficulties?

- How are the suffering and glory of Christ related to the suffering and glory of Christians?

  If you are in a group, ask the members how they respond to this connection between their experience and what Jesus experienced. Ask: How does it change the way you think and feel about your trials?

PRAYER

Commit what you have learned from God's Word in this lesson to prayer.

- Praise God for His eternal and glorious purpose in our suffering.
- Confess any ways that you have responded to suffering with doubt or bitterness.
- Thank God for the resurrection of Christ, which puts all our suffering in perspective.
- Ask God for patience, gentleness, and joy as you endure trials.

REVIEW QUIZ

Use these multiple-choice questions to measure what you learned from this lesson.

1. How should Christians interpret their suffering? Through what lens should they look?
   a. Their feelings
   b. Their past
   c. The fruit of their suffering
   d. God's Word

2. When Christians see their suffering in its proper gospel context, what will they do?
   a. Embrace their pain
   b. Examine their hearts
   c. Rejoice
   d. Focus on obedience

3. When Christians see their suffering in its proper context, they will not grieve.
   a. True
   b. False

4. What historical event reveals the gospel's glory as we suffer?
   a. The birth of Jesus
   b. Pentecost
   c. The Last Supper
   d. The resurrection

5. Peter refers to the book of Job to show that God allows Christians to suffer in order to test what?
   a. Their obedience
   b. Their faith
   c. Their knowledge
   d. Their spiritual gifts

6. When Christians suffer, God is treating them the same way he treated whom?
   a. Adam
   b. King Saul
   c. Jesus
   d. John the Baptist

Answer Key—Glory in Our Grief

REFLECTION & DISCUSSION QUESTIONS

Before the Video

What Do You Think?

These are personal questions. The answers should be based on your own knowledge and experience.

Scripture Reading

- How is God identified by the Apostle Paul in this passage? What does God do for us when we suffer? Why does He do this?

  Paul identifies God as the "Father of our Lord Jesus Christ," the "Father of mercies," and the "God of all comfort." God comforts His suffering people. He does this so that those He comforts can comfort others in the same way. As Christians, we share in both Christ's sufferings and His comfort.

During the Video

What Comforts the Christian?

- How does Satan want Christians to interpret their suffering?

  At the end of the letter, Peter refers to Satan's strategies against the church. In particular, Satan wants Christians to interpret their suffering by what they feel instead of by what God has said in the Bible. We need to let God teach us in His Word what our suffering means.

- What comforting words did Jesus speak in John 17?

  In His High Priestly Prayer, Jesus said, "I have guarded them, and not one of them has been lost" (John 17:12). Jesus keeps His disciples secure. He prays for all Christians, and since the Father always listens to His prayers, no Christian will be separated from Him. Even in suffering, we can find comfort when we remember that none will be lost.

The Purpose of Christian Suffering

- What is the purpose of trials in the Christian life?

  In God's providence, all the trials that Christians endure have a purpose. Knowing this can make all the difference. God's purpose in our trials is to test His workmanship (1 Peter 1:7; see also Job 23:10). He is forming us into new people who will reflect His glory, and trials reveal what He has done in us.

- What blessings does God want us to experience even while we suffer?

  As we are tested and endure by looking to Christ, our faith grows more stable. Our suffering causes us to look to Christ and rejoice. In these ways, we already experience the glory of our inheritance.

- Aside from Christians, who else sees the glory of the gospel?

  Peter tells these Christians that the gospel is so glorious that even angels want to see it. Even heavenly beings know that the gospel is extraordinary. The Old Testament prophets who foretold Christ's coming did not fully understand the gospel. Now, though, the suffering and glory of Christ have been fully revealed in history.

After the Video

- How does Peter comfort these Christians? How is this like or unlike other common ways of offering comfort?

  Peter comforts his readers by reminding them of the glory of the gospel. He reminds them how glorious it is to be a child of God, a disciple of Jesus Christ, and one in whom the Holy Spirit works. Rather than saying, "I feel your pain," he directs their attention away from their pain to these eternal blessings that God has given them. This transforms their suffering.

- What is the inheritance of Christians? Why does Peter say that it is glorious?

  As children of God, Christians have an eternal inheritance. We have already been born again—spiritually resurrected—through the Holy Spirit. One day, our bodies will be resurrected, just as God the Father raised Christ from the dead. This inheritance is guarded by God Himself and cannot be lost.

- How are the suffering and glory of Christ related to the suffering and glory of Christians?

  Through His suffering and death, Jesus Christ paid for our sins. This led to the glory of the resurrection, the victory over death. Those who put their faith in Christ are united to Him in His suffering and in His glorious resurrection. Our lives, then, follow the same pattern: suffering and then glory.

REVIEW QUIZ

1. **D.**
   Our beliefs about the meaning and purpose of our suffering will affect how we experience our trials. Instead of believing our feelings, we must look to God's Word to tell us the meaning of our suffering.

2. **C.**
   When Christians see their suffering in the context of the gospel, they rejoice. The glory of the gospel is so great that our trials seem light by comparison. It may also

lead us to examine our hearts or strengthen our resolve to obey, but these responses are not the main point of the passage studied in this lesson.

3. **B.**
   Although the gospel enables us to rejoice and endure trials, it does not take away grief. We rejoice and experience glory in the midst of our grief.

4. **D.**
   The resurrection of Christ, a past event, points us to our future resurrection. Christ's resurrection is God's decisive triumph over sin and death, and the guarantee of our future triumph.

5. **B.**
   Through suffering, our faith becomes more obvious, and it is strengthened. Job said, "When he has tried me, I shall come out as gold" (Job 23:10). This precious outcome is one of God's purposes for our suffering.

6. **C.**
   As Christ entered into glory by the path of suffering, so it is with Christians. We are united to Christ by faith, and by faith we share in both His suffering and His glory.

3

Do We Belong Here?

INTRODUCTION

It is not strange for Christians to find themselves marginalized by society. We do not belong here. We are sojourners and exiles whose true home is in heaven. This heavenly citizenship gives us our identity, our hope, and our guidance regarding how to live. In this lesson, Dr. Ferguson describes the "grammar of the gospel," principles rooted in the gospel that guide Christian sojourners and exiles living on earth.

LEARNING GOALS

When you have finished this lesson, you should be able to:

- Describe the outline of 1 Peter
- Explain why Peter refers to Christians as exiles
- Understand the "grammar of the gospel" in 1 Peter 1:13–21

KEY IDEAS

- Christians belong to the kingdom of God, so they live in earthly society as exiles.
- The gospel renews our minds, as illustrated by six principles described in this passage.

REFLECTION & DISCUSSION QUESTIONS

Before the Video

What Do You Think?

Take a moment to answer the following questions. They will prepare you for the lecture.

- Where do you feel that you really belong? What do you think of as your home?

- Do you think of the gospel as logical or mainly as an emotional or intuitive reality? Why?

Scripture Reading

> *But our citizenship is in heaven, and from it we await a Savior, the Lord Jesus Christ, who will transform our lowly body to be like his glorious body, by the power that enables him even to subject all things to himself.*
>
> —Philippians 3:20–21

- Where is our primary citizenship? Who is our King? According to this passage, what do we do during our earthly life?

During the Video

Answer the following questions while you watch the video. They will guide you through the lecture.

The Christian Accent *0:00–12:00*

- What two calls form the core of 1 Peter?

- How does the heavenly citizenship of Christians inevitably affect Christian identity on earth?

- What are the first two principles of the grammar of the gospel?

Children of God *12:00–25:03*

- What are the third and fourth principles of the grammar of the gospel?

- What are the fifth and sixth principles of the grammar of the gospel?

After the Video

Answer the following questions after you have finished the lecture. They will help you identify and summarize the major points.

- How can the structure of 1 Peter be summarized? What is its outline?

  If you are in a group, have the members discuss why they think knowing the letter's outline matters. Ask: How can understanding the overall shape and content of the letter help you understand its message and its individual parts?

- What is the role of the mind in Christian faith?

  If you are in a group, have the members discuss whether knowledge of the gospel and its logic has shaped any of their decisions or actions in the previous week. Ask: How do you see the gospel renewing your mind?

- Which of the six principles described in this lesson help us understand our identity as Christians? How?

  If you are in a group, have the members name other aspects of their personal identities (parent, child, employee, manager, citizen, etc.). Ask: How do these different identities relate to your identity as a Christian?

PRAYER

Commit what you have learned from God's Word in this lesson to prayer.

- Praise God for an identity in Christ that is glorious and secure.
- Confess any ways that you try to hide your heavenly citizenship.
- Thank God for renewing your mind through the Holy Spirit's application of the gospel.
- Ask God to help you focus on the glorious future that we await as Christians.

REVIEW QUIZ

Use these multiple-choice questions to measure what you learned from this lesson.

1. What is true the greater the indicatives of the gospel?
   a. The more relaxed the imperatives
   b. The more rigorous the imperatives
   c. The more complex the imperatives
   d. The more confusing the imperatives

2. Our lifestyle is always the fruit of what?
   a. Our feelings
   b. Our culture
   c. Our mindset
   d. Our childhood

3. Our lives as Christians are defined mostly by what?
   a. Our past
   b. Our present
   c. Our future
   d. Our income

4. What determines whom we are called to become as Christians?
   a. Our family
   b. Our church
   c. Our spiritual gifts
   d. Our God

5. In the Christian life, what did Dr. Ferguson say must always be balanced?
   a. The law and the gospel
   b. The positive and the negative
   c. Faith and works
   d. Success and humility

6. As children of God, we should be characterized by what in our lives?
   a. Fear
   b. Flair
   c. Timidity
   d. Ambition

Answer Key—Do We Belong Here?

REFLECTION & DISCUSSION QUESTIONS

Before the Video

What Do You Think?

These are personal questions. The answers should be based on your own knowledge and experience.

Scripture Reading

- Where is our primary citizenship? Who is our King? According to this passage, what do we do during our earthly life?

  This passage says that our citizenship is in heaven. Jesus is our King. He is Lord, and He rules everything. The Apostle describes Christians, therefore, as people who wait. Our lives are guided by the eager expectation of Christ's return and the resurrection of our bodies through His sovereign power. These events, which happen together, are the fulfillment of our deepest hopes.

During the Video

The Christian Accent

- What two calls form the core of 1 Peter?

  The core of the letter is first the call to be holy (1:13–3:7) and second the call to suffer as those who are godly (3:8–4:9). Together, these calls show what Christian life on earth ought to be. This lesson, which focuses on 1 Peter 1:13–21, covers the first part of the first of these calls.

- How does the heavenly citizenship of Christians inevitably affect Christian identity on earth?

  Christians' heavenly citizenship will inevitably make them different from other people. This difference will be noticeable to others, the way that an accent tells others where you are from. For Christians, our way of life shows that we belong to another kingdom.

- What are the first two principles of the grammar of the gospel?

  The "grammar of the gospel" refers to the basic logic of life for those who belong to Christ's kingdom. The first principle of this grammar that the passage describes is that all imperative statements are based on indicative statements. Imperatives are commands—what should be done. Indicatives declare the true state of things. So in the gospel, all that we must do (imperatives) is the result of the salvation that we already have in Christ (indicatives) and not vice versa. The second principle is that our lifestyle is always the fruit of our mindset: how we think shapes how we live.

Children of God

- What are the third and fourth principles of the grammar of the gospel?

  The third principle is that our present life is rooted in future grace. Our lives are mainly shaped by our focus on our glorious future, when Christ will return and our bodies will be raised. The fourth principle is that God determines what we are called to be. We are called to be holy because He is holy.

- What are the fifth and sixth principles of the grammar of the gospel?

  The fifth principle is that negative activity must always be balanced by positive activity. We need to turn away from sin, but we also need to "put on" Christ, living out His holiness. The sixth principle is that Christians' new identity in Christ determines how they live. Through the gospel, we are children of God, and our knowing this shapes our lives.

After the Video

- How can the structure of 1 Peter be summarized? What is its outline?

  The bookends of 1 Peter are the opening and closing greetings (1:1–2; 5:12–14). First Peter 1:3–12 is a doxology—a hymn of praise. Toward the end, Peter encourages his readers to live with one another in humility (4:10–5:11). The core or spine of the letter—its main content—consists of calls to be holy (1:13–3:7) and to suffer as those who are godly (3:8–4:9).

- What is the role of the mind in Christian faith?

  The grammar of the gospel that this passage describes reflects the fact that Christian faith involves thinking. The gospel is not determined by our feelings. The Bible is not a book of random promises. It is a book of logic, as the word "therefore" at the beginning of this passage indicates. The gospel is the truth about what God has done for us in Christ, and it changes us by renewing our minds.

- Which of the six principles described in this lesson help us understand our identity as Christians? How?

  All the principles help us know who we are. The first principle tells us that we are those who obey God because of what Christ has already done for us. The second tells us that we are those whose minds are being transformed by the Word of God. According to the third principle, we are defined by expectation of a glorious future rather than our past accomplishments or failures. The fourth through sixth principles all, in different ways, tell us that we are children of God, called to reflect His character.

REVIEW QUIZ

1. **B.**
   The gospel does not make God's law easier to obey. Instead, the knowledge that we are already justified through Christ's blood frees us from sin and enables us to obey God's will. In this life, our obedience is always imperfect, but we are called to be holy and not to live as the unbelieving world does.

2. **C.**
   Peter calls his readers to prepare their minds because our thinking will determine our actions (1 Peter 1:13). Our minds are often corrupted by the world's patterns of thought, which cause us to live contrary to the gospel. God's Word renews our minds, which changes our lives.

3. **C.**
   Christians live in hope of future grace and glory. We look back to Christ's death and resurrection in order to know how we have been reconciled to God. We look ahead, though, to when we will see Christ face-to-face and will be raised from the dead. This hope encourages and comforts us now in our time of exile.

4. **D.**
   We are called by God, so we are called to become like God in our character. He is holy, so we must be holy (1 Peter 1:15–16). God's own character is the basis of His commands to us. As our Father, He calls us to reflect His image.

5. **B.**
   In the Christian life, the negative must always be balanced with the positive, and the positive must always be balanced with the negative. We need to put our sin to death. At the same time, we need to grow in holiness by putting on Christ.

6. **A.**
   Peter says to those who call on God as Father, "Conduct yourselves with fear throughout the time of your exile" (1 Peter 1:17). This is not a fear of punishment. It is the fear of displeasing One we love and revere, who made us His children through the precious blood of His eternal Son, Jesus.

4

A Love the World Wants

INTRODUCTION

Christians have been born again and are now part of God's family. That new identity gives them a new relationship with God. It also gives them a new relationship to other Christians, who are now their brothers and sisters. In this lesson, Dr. Ferguson shows how brotherly love in the church is the anchor for living a faithful Christian life in a hostile society.

LEARNING GOALS

When you have finished this lesson, you should be able to:

- Describe the nature of the church, the new community that God has created by His Spirit
- Explain the distinctive characteristics of Christian love and unity
- Understand how the church grows in brotherly love

KEY IDEAS

- Christians' love for one another is family love that flows from our new birth.
- Love in the church begins with the knowledge that other Christians are our brothers and sisters because Christ died for them.
- Christians grow in their love for one another as the Word of God renews their minds.

REFLECTION & DISCUSSION QUESTIONS

Before the Video

What Do You Think?

Take a moment to answer the following questions. They will prepare you for the lecture.

- What makes the church a unique community? What characteristics of the church's fellowship make it different from other communities?

- What is the main way that the gospel spreads? How do you think Christians should evangelize the world?

Scripture Reading

I do not ask for these only, but also for those who will believe in me through their word, that they may all be one, just as you, Father, are in me, and I in you, that they also may be in us, so that the world may believe that you have sent me.

—John 17:20–21

- Who does Jesus pray will be united? What will be the result of this unity?

During the Video

Answer the following questions while you watch the video. They will guide you through the lecture.

What Is Christian Love? *0:00–12:28*

- What kind of love does Peter exhort Christians to show?

- Is Christian love more a matter of feelings or of the mind?

Where Does Christian Love Come From? *12:28–24:57*

- What is the precondition of Christian love?

- What inspires Christian love?

- What spiritual food do we need to love others in the church?

After the Video

Answer the following questions after you have finished the lecture. They will help you identify and summarize the major points.

- What is the relationship between the church community and our individual sanctification?

  If you are in a group, have the members discuss what they think has most contributed to their spiritual growth. Ask: How has the presence or absence of brotherly love in the church affected your sanctification?

- What is the relationship between truth and actions in the Christian life?

  If you are in a group, have the members offer examples of how understanding or remembering a truth in Scripture helped them act in a more loving way. Ask: Do you tend to associate Christian love more with truth or with feelings?

- How does brotherly love in the church relate to those outside the church?

  If you are in a group, have the members describe how non-Christians they know think about the church. Ask: In your experience, how much does the church community tend to be seen positively by outsiders?

PRAYER

Commit what you have learned from God's Word in this lesson to prayer.

- Praise God because He is the God of love who wants us to reflect His love.
- Confess any lack of love in your heart toward other Christians.
- Thank God for the church, the spiritual family He has given us through the death of His Son.
- Ask God to help you see fellow Christians more clearly as brothers and sisters, so that this truth can increase your love toward them.

REVIEW QUIZ

Use these multiple-choice questions to measure what you learned from this lesson.

1. In the New Testament, what does the gospel mainly spread through?
   a. Apologetics
   b. Individual evangelism
   c. Persecution
   d. The witness of the church community
2. Which American city is named after the kind of love that Peter describes in this passage?
   a. Albuquerque
   b. Memphis
   c. Philadelphia
   d. Pittsburgh
3. Which of the following is *not* an example of groups who find unity with each other in the church?
   a. The repentant and the unrepentant
   b. The rich and the poor
   c. The wise and the simple
   d. The old and the young
4. What does Peter call the Bible?
   a. Spiritual meat
   b. Spiritual wine
   c. Spiritual water
   d. Spiritual milk
5. God cares more about our obedience than our understanding.
   a. True
   b. False
6. What is *not* true about Christian brotherly love?
   a. It is an inevitable fruit of regeneration.
   b. It is something that Christians strive for.
   c. It is attractive to non-Christians.
   d. It is possible for non-Christians.

Answer Key—A Love the World Wants

REFLECTION & DISCUSSION QUESTIONS

Before the Video

What Do You Think?

These are personal questions. The answers should be based on your own knowledge and experience.

Scripture Reading

- Who does Jesus pray will be united? What will be the result of this unity?

  Jesus prays for Christians to be united to one another as they are each united to Christ and Christ is united to the Father. This oneness is a witness to the world of the gospel, that the Father sent the Son to be the Savior of the world.

During the Video

What Is Christian Love?

- What kind of love does Peter exhort Christians to show?

  Peter exhorts them to practice philadelphia, *"brotherly love" (1 Peter 1:22). Like love for one's natural family, this love is instinctive. It is the fruit of regeneration that becomes "natural" to show to our Christian family in a sincere and genuine way.*

- Is Christian love more a matter of feelings or of the mind?

  Christian love should be earnest and fervent, but it is not mainly a feeling. It is principally a matter of how we think about one another. The idea that love is not primarily a matter of emotion is conveyed in the very fact that love is commanded of us.

Where Does Christian Love Come From?

- What is the precondition of Christian love?

  The precondition of Christian love is knowledge of the truth that other Christians are one's brothers and sisters. Seeing others as family revolutionizes our view of them. We see them as those for whom Jesus gave His precious blood.

- What inspires Christian love?

  The new birth, or regeneration, inspires Christian love. As those who are born again, we are adopted into a new family, and other Christians are our brothers and sisters. Our new nature gives us new instincts toward others. It also renews our minds, helping us to see others in a new way.

- What spiritual food do we need in order to love others in the church?

  In order to love our brothers and sisters in the church, we need the "pure spiritual milk" of the Word of God (1 Peter 2:2). We should desire this spiritual food, which is the only nourishment that can give us the strength and understanding to love.

After the Video

- What is the relationship between the church community and our individual sanctification?

  When we are born again, we become part of God's family, spiritually related to other Christians. This new birth inspires love toward our spiritual brothers and sisters. These family relationships are where we should first see the fruit of the Holy Spirit's work in our lives, and they are the main context for our ongoing growth in love and holiness.

- What is the relationship between truth and actions in the Christian life?

  Christians are born again through the Word of God, the Bible, where they hear the good news of Christ's death for sinners. The Word of God is also the means by which we grow in Christian character. Therefore, feelings or intuitions are not the main source of loving actions, but the renewing of our minds through the truth of the Scriptures. A deepening understanding of God and the gospel transforms our lives over time.

- How does brotherly love in the church relate to those outside the church?

  First, family love in the church strengthens the church and helps Christians endure the hostility that they may face from unbelievers. Second, this love shows the world that God lives among His people. The love and unity of the church can be a powerful witness and attraction to unbelievers.

REVIEW QUIZ

1. **D.**
   Apologetics, individual evangelism, and persecution have all contributed to the church's growth over the centuries. But the New Testament, in texts such as John 17, emphasizes the witness of the church's love and unity.

2. **C.**
   The Greek word philadelphia *combines* philos *(love) and* adelphos *(brother). Peter uses this word here instead of other Greek words for "love."*

3. **A.**
   The New Testament describes how all kinds of groups that are often at odds in the world come together in the church. The unwillingness to repent, however, creates and sustains division.

4. **D.**
   Peter tells his readers that they should desire the Bible the way that newborn babies desire milk. This milk will nourish them and enable them to grow.

5. **B.**
   Obedience and understanding are not in tension. God renews our minds through His Word. This deepens our understanding, which is the basis of our obedience. The Holy Spirit, who illumines our minds to understand the Bible, also empowers us to obey the Bible. We cannot, for example, show brotherly love toward other Christians without understanding that they are our brothers and sisters through Christ's death.

6. **D.**
   Brotherly love in the church is both an inevitable result of the new birth and something that Christians strive for. Non-Christians can find the family love of the church attractive, but they cannot practice it without the illumination and empowerment of the Holy Spirit, who gives new life to sinners and illumines their minds to understand the Word.

5

The Royal Family

INTRODUCTION

The church is God's family, and it grows together in brotherly love. But why? What is the church for? Peter says that the church is God's temple, chosen race, royal priesthood, and holy nation. In this lesson, Dr. Ferguson shows how these images, all drawn from the Old Testament, teach us that God's purpose for His people is to reflect His glory.

LEARNING GOALS

When you have finished this lesson, you should be able to:

- Explain why Peter calls the church God's temple
- Understand what the phrases "chosen race," "royal priesthood," and "holy nation" mean
- Describe the purpose of the church

KEY IDEAS

- The church is now God's temple, the place where God lives, and it is built on the foundation of Christ.
- The church is a distinct people, chosen and honored by God.
- Christ builds His church so that the church will display God's character to the world.

REFLECTION & DISCUSSION QUESTIONS

Before the Video

What Do You Think?

Take a moment to answer the following questions. They will prepare you for the lecture.

- Does your church have a mission statement? If so, what is it? What do you think is the church's purpose in the world?

- What is your understanding of the Old Testament temple and priesthood? What purpose did they serve? How are they related to Christ and the new covenant church?

Scripture Reading

Then Peter, filled with the Holy Spirit, said to them, "Rulers of the people and elders, if we are being examined today concerning a good deed done to a crippled man, by what means this man has been healed, let it be known to all of you and to all the people of Israel that by the name of Jesus Christ of Nazareth, whom you crucified, whom God raised from the dead—by him this man is standing before you well. This Jesus is the stone that was rejected by you, the builders, which has become the cornerstone. And there is salvation in no one else, for there is no other name under heaven given among men by which we must be saved."

—Acts 4:8–12

- To whom is Peter speaking in this passage? What is their relationship to Jesus and His temple? Does Peter refer to the church in this speech?

During the Video

Answer the following questions while you watch the video. They will guide you through the lecture.

What Is God's Temple? *0:00–12:13*

- What is the glue that holds God's temple, the church, together?

- What gives the church its dignity?

The Purpose of the Church *12:13–24:02*

- Why is the church a new kind of priesthood?

- Since we are part of God's family through Christ, what can we call God?

- What is the secret of the life of the church?

After the Video

Answer the following questions after you have finished the lecture. They will help you identify and summarize the major points.

- How does Jesus build His temple? What are all the aspects of this process?

  If you are in a group, have the members discuss how they respond to the imagery of the temple. Ask: Does it seem foreign or archaic? How does this image help you see your union with Christ and His church differently?

- Why is love necessary for the building of Christ's church?

  If you are in a group, have the members discuss whether they tend to think that unity with other Christians is hard. Ask: How much time do you spend with Christians who are different from you or seem like difficult people?

- God is building His temple for His glory, but what does this mean? What is God's glory, and how does the church bring it about?

  If you are in a group, have the members discuss whether they usually think of Christian virtues as reflections of God's attributes. Ask: How does thinking of the church's glory in this way affect how you think of yourself as a Christian?

PRAYER

Commit what you have learned from God's Word in this lesson to prayer.

- Praise God for building His people into a holy temple through Christ.
- Confess any reluctance you feel to love certain members of your church.
- Thank God for the honor of displaying His glory.
- Ask God to bring greater unity to your church and the universal church.

REVIEW QUIZ

Use these multiple-choice questions to measure what you learned from this lesson.

1. What will we have if we belong to the church, according to 1 Peter 2:4–12?
   a. Fame
   b. Honor
   c. Success
   d. Power
2. In order to build God's temple, we should find those who are like-minded or easy to work with.
   a. True
   b. False
3. How must we see other Christians if our attitudes toward each other are to be changed?
   a. As free
   b. As chosen
   c. As gifted
   d. As good
4. Which of the following is *not* a characteristic of God that the church reflects?
   a. Holiness
   b. Wisdom
   c. Faithfulness
   d. Omniscience
5. What caused God to choose those whom He makes part of His church?
   a. Their faith
   b. His justice
   c. Their repentance
   d. His love
6. Which of the following is *not* a way that the world will respond to the church?
   a. Recognition of the church's good deeds
   b. Confusion
   c. Understanding
   d. Hostility

Answer Key—The Royal Family

REFLECTION & DISCUSSION QUESTIONS

Before the Video

What Do You Think?

These are personal questions. The answers should be based on your own knowledge and experience.

Scripture Reading

- To whom is Peter speaking in this passage? What is their relationship to Jesus and His temple? Does Peter refer to the church in this speech?

  In this passage, Peter addresses the rulers of Israel. He calls them "the builders," which shows that they ought to recognize Jesus and build God's temple on Him. Instead, they rejected Jesus, the cornerstone of the temple. Through Jesus, God brings salvation to everyone who believes the gospel. These believers are the church, God's true temple.

During the Video

What Is God's Temple?

- What is the glue that holds God's temple, the church, together?

  The glue or concrete that holds the church together is love. God often does not unite people who have common interests or other natural affinities. The "living stones" who constitute God's temple are sinners who by nature would not want to tolerate one another. The love of Christ overcomes all these antagonisms to create a unified structure.

- What gives the church its dignity?

  Our dignity does not depend on ourselves. It depends on the fact that God has chosen us. What separates the church from the world is not any natural or worldly privileges or accomplishments.

The Purpose of the Church

- Why is the church a new kind of priesthood?

  In the Old Testament, Israel's kings and priests came from different family lines. No one could ever hold both offices. The church, though, is a royal priesthood. We are priests, and we are members of the King's family.

- Since we are part of God's family through Christ, what can we call God?

Since Christians belong to God's family, we can call the King "Abba, Father." Calling God "Father" reflects the intimate relationship that we now have with Him through Christ.

- What is the secret of the life of the church?

  The secret of the life of the church is that we are the Lord's possession. Christians belong to Jesus, and Jesus belongs to them. This is why Christians are a chosen race, a royal priesthood, and a holy nation.

After the Video

- How does Jesus build His temple? What are all the aspects of this process?

  Jesus builds His temple, first, through his death. He is the "living stone rejected by men" (1 Peter 2:4) whom God chose to save His people. Through faith in Him, we are united to Him and become living stones like Him (2:5). Christ continues to build His temple through love that strengthens the structure and attracts new members.

- Why is love necessary for the building of Christ's church?

  Love is necessary in order to build God's church because the members do not naturally fit together. God makes His temple out of living stones from every ethnicity, personality type, and background. All these stones are sinners, and earthly binding agents, such as blood ties and common interests, are inadequate. Only love, the gift of the Holy Spirit, can overcome all our natural tendencies and make a stable, unified structure that glorifies God.

- God is building His temple for His glory, but what does this mean? What is God's glory, and how does the church bring it about?

  God builds His temple so that the church, His redeemed people, can "proclaim the excellencies" of the One who saved them (1 Peter 2:9). The church, especially in its common life, displays all the glorious attributes of God, so that He is known and praised. God made Christians part of His family to know and be like Him.

REVIEW QUIZ

1. **B.**
   The church has spiritual power through the Holy Spirit that dwells among God's people, but the emphasis in this passage is the honor of the church. Christians receive honor not for their own glorious deeds but instead because they believe in Christ and now belong to God's royal family.

2. **B.**
   Christ builds His temple out of a great diversity of people, many of whom do not naturally get along. Differences in the church may result from age, race, gender, or class, but they often are just a result of divergent personalities and priorities and human selfishness. That is why love is the necessary glue of the temple.

3. **B.**
   Christians recognize one another as those chosen by God. This changes how they see one another. Whatever differences might naturally exist among us, we know that the essential reality is that we have all been chosen by God for the glorious blessings of salvation.

4. **D.**
   God wants His church to reflect all His communicable attributes, such as holiness, goodness, wisdom, faithfulness, and perseverance. These are the characteristics of God that humans can share or reflect. The church will not reflect God's incommunicable attributes, such as omniscience (having all knowledge) and omnipotence (having all power).

5. **D.**
   God chose people to be members of His church before He created the world. He did not choose them because He foresaw their faith or repentance. He did not choose them because of their characteristics or actions. He chose them purely out of love.

6. **C.**
   The world may acknowledge the good deeds of the church, but it will not understand the church. As a chosen race, citizens of God's kingdom, and the adopted children of God, Christians have an identity that does not fit within the world's reasoning.

6

Living in Two Worlds

INTRODUCTION

Christians live in two worlds. We are citizens of heaven, but we are still on earth. We are called to love our brothers and sisters in the church, but Christ also calls us to serve Him in our vocations in the world. In this lesson, Dr. Ferguson helps us understand that through the gospel, we are servants and yet free in Christ as we live within the broken structures of earthly society.

LEARNING GOALS

When you have finished this lesson, you should be able to:

- Describe how faith in Christ calls us and enables us to serve society
- Understand the nature of Christian liberty

KEY IDEAS

- Christians must live in submission to earthly authorities in order to do good in society.
- Christians are free from sin and free in their earthly service because their Master is Christ.
- By submitting in our vocations, we follow the model of Christ.

REFLECTION & DISCUSSION QUESTIONS

Before the Video

What Do You Think?

Take a moment to answer the following questions. They will prepare you for the lecture.

- How do you feel about your government (local, state, or national)? In what ways do you believe that you must submit to it?

- In what sense do you believe that being a Christian makes you free? How does this freedom affect the way you live?

Scripture Reading

> *I do not ask that you take them out of the world, but that you keep them from the evil one. They are not of the world, just as I am not of the world. Sanctify them in the truth; your word is truth. As you sent me into the world, so I have sent them into the world.*
>
> —John 17:15–18

- What does Jesus pray for in these verses? What does this prayer tell us about Christians' identity and how we should live?

During the Video

Answer the following questions while you watch the video. They will guide you through the lecture.

Servants of Society *0:00–14:26*

- Does 1 Peter imply that a certain form of human government is best?

- What is the source of human governments?

- What country did Dr. Ferguson describe as an example of modern Christians' submitting to a totalitarian government?

Servants of Christ *14:26–25:15*

- How is Christ an example to us of living in human society?

- What is the ultimate evidence that you are really free?

After the Video

Answer the following questions after you have finished the lecture. They will help you identify and summarize the major points.

- What are the two elements of Christian life and identity that help us understand how to live in a hostile world?

  If you are in a group, have the members discuss whether they respond differently to being children of God and being servants of Christ. Ask: What thoughts and feelings does each image provoke? In what concrete situations have either of these ideas helped you?

- Why does God want us to submit to earthly leaders or masters?

  If you are in a group, have the members discuss how they can live submissively in their specific vocations. Ask: In what situations does it seem especially difficult? Can you imagine situations in which submission to authority might support evil? If so, how might Christians consider such situations in light of this passage?

- What is Christian liberty?

  If you are in a group, have the members describe what hopes and desires are aroused when they hear the word *liberty*. Ask: How well do these desires fit with the idea of Christian liberty explained in this lesson?

PRAYER

Commit what you have learned from God's Word in this lesson to prayer.

- Praise God for showing us the ultimate model of humility and submission in Jesus.
- Confess ways that you resist submission to authority.
- Thank God for the freedom from sin and death that He gives us through the gospel.
- Ask God to help you look to the model of Jesus' submission, so that you can joyfully serve society.

REVIEW QUIZ

Use these multiple-choice questions to measure what you learned from this lesson.

1. Which forms of government can a Christian faithfully obey?
   a. Liberal democracy
   b. Totalitarianism
   c. Mixed monarchy
   d. All of the above

2. As Christians, what do we no longer have?
   a. Earthly citizenship
   b. Concern for society
   c. Inalienable rights
   d. Political beliefs

3. If we are persecuted or demeaned as Christians, it is ultimately because people oppose what?
   a. Our politics
   b. Religion
   c. Our good works
   d. Christ

4. What historical institution do modern readers often believe that Peter should have condemned?
   a. The Roman Senate
   b. Slavery
   c. Gladiatorial games
   d. Pagan schools

5. Peter's main pastoral concern is to help Christians live faithfully regardless of what?
   a. Their health
   b. Their church's beliefs
   c. Their circumstances
   d. Their ethnicity

6. According to the lesson, what do Christians come to understand better when they suffer?
   a. Christ's suffering
   b. Political power
   c. God's transcendence
   d. The nature of the soul

Answer Key—Living in Two Worlds

REFLECTION & DISCUSSION QUESTIONS

Before the Video

What Do You Think?

These are personal questions. The answers should be based on your own knowledge and experience.

Scripture Reading

- What does Jesus pray for in these verses? What does this prayer tell us about Christians' identity and how we should live?

  Jesus prays that God the Father will protect the church from Satan. Like Jesus, Christians are in the world but not of the world. Jesus sends His church into the world, but He asks the Father to sanctify its members or set them apart from the world. Christians live on earth as a distinct people whose home is elsewhere, and they need God's protection.

During the Video

Servants of Society

- Does 1 Peter imply that a certain form of human government is best?

  No. Peter lived in a pagan empire that at times persecuted Christians, but he does not say anything about desiring another form of government. Instead, he tells his readers to submit to the emperor. His instructions, then, apply to any form of government that Christians might live under.

- What is the source of human governments?

  God is the source of human governments. Humans create particular forms of government, but human government is ordained by God and exists under His providential rule.

- What country did Dr. Ferguson describe as an example of modern Christians' submitting to a totalitarian government?

  Dr. Ferguson mentioned Romania, when it was under communist rule, as an example of a modern tyrannical state in which Christians lived and served. Christians were violently persecuted at times and yet sought to be the most faithful citizens in Romanian society. This oppressive human government did not prevent Christians from living in obedience to Christ.

Servants of Christ

- How is Christ an example to us of living in human society?

  Jesus did not protest oppression. He said nothing as He went to the cross. He knew that His obedience would bring glory to His Father. Likewise, we are called to submit to earthly leaders in order to glorify God through our service.

- What is the ultimate evidence that you are really free?

  The ultimate evidence that you are really free is that you seek to do good and serve society under any government. It is not the leaders who control your ability to do good. Christ makes us free to serve Him anywhere and at any time.

After the Video

- What are the two elements of Christian life and identity that help us understand how to live in a hostile world?

  Christians are both children of God and servants of the Lord Jesus Christ. Therefore, we have all the freedom and privileges of being part of God's family and yet also obey Christ, who commands us to submit to others. When we grasp both these principles, we see how service to Christ is freedom and how we can be citizens of heaven even if we are in bondage on earth.

- Why does God want us to submit to earthly leaders or masters?

  God wants us to submit to authorities in order to do good to society through our vocations. Ultimately, such submission helps the gospel prosper, whereas rebellion or poor citizenship undermines the gospel. In a way that seems paradoxical, our submission to earthly authorities shows that we are free, since our earthly obedience is an acknowledgment of Christ's ultimate authority in our lives.

- What is Christian liberty?

  While the political freedoms that we may enjoy are gifts from God, they are not gospel freedom. Christian freedom comes from our citizenship in heaven. Since Christ has freed us from sin and judgment through His death, we are free to serve everyone for His sake. As we live on earth, we do so with the knowledge that we belong to another kingdom, that we are children of God, and that the human rulers whom we serve are not our ultimate authorities.

REVIEW QUIZ

1. **D.**
   Human beings form different structures of government, and Christians are called to submit to their government regardless of its form. Christ is our Lord, and He is above all human rulers. We show our loyalty to Him by obeying His command to serve the government that God, in His providence, has placed us under.

2. **C.**
   As Christians, we do not lose our political citizenship, and it is good for us to form political beliefs that are wise and just. Rather than losing our concern for society, we are called to be our country's best citizens. Our political and social concerns are not, however, based on defending our own inalienable rights. For the sake of the gospel, we willingly give these up.

3. **D.**
   If we are seeking to submit to Christ, we can know that hostility toward us ultimately comes from hostility toward Him. Non-Christians are not necessarily against our good works, which may benefit them. They are not necessarily against religion, which is a vital part of most societies. They are opposed to Christ.

4. **B.**
   Peter's instructions to slaves can be especially troubling to modern people who live after the era of chattel slavery in the West. Peter, though, does not intend to either condemn or defend the institution of slavery. Instead, he wants Christians to see that no human institution can keep them from serving Christ. To teach and encourage us, he points to Christ as the model of servanthood (1 Peter 2:21).

5. **C.**
   Peter wants to encourage and comfort Christians by reminding them that their circumstances cannot separate them from Christ or keep them from serving Him. In fact, oppression can even be a means by which God draws us closer to Him and strengthens our faith.

6. **A.**
   As Christians, we know that Christ died for our sins. This is why we are children of God and look forward in hope to the resurrection. But as we experience suffering for Christ's sake, we gain a deeper, fuller understanding of our Savior and what He has done to save us.

7

Returning to Eden

INTRODUCTION

Peter teaches that the gospel works in every situation. It calls for brotherly love in the church and submission in society. Now Peter shows how gospel service shapes marriage—the original human society. In this lesson, Dr. Ferguson explains that submission in the home for the sake of Christ, even when one's spouse is not a Christian, can bring glory to Christ and advance the gospel.

LEARNING GOALS

When you have finished this lesson, you should be able to:

- Explain how the gospel guides husbands and wives
- Understand why Peter addresses wives more than husbands
- Describe how Christians can best present the gospel to their families

KEY IDEAS

- Christians must submit themselves to each other in marriage, for the glory of Christ.
- Christians married to non-Christians can best make the gospel known through their way of life.
- Christian husbands must honor their wives as fellow heirs of eternal life.

REFLECTION & DISCUSSION QUESTIONS

Before the Video

What Do You Think?

Take a moment to answer the following questions. They will prepare you for the lecture.

- What do you believe makes a good Christian marriage? What models of marriage do you look to for guidance?

Scripture Reading

> *Therefore a man shall leave his father and his mother and hold fast to his wife, and they shall become one flesh. And the man and his wife were both naked and were not ashamed.*
>
> —Genesis 2:24–25

- How would you describe this original picture of marriage before Adam and Eve sinned? Does it have any relevance to Christian marriages today? Why or why not?

During the Video

Answer the following questions while you watch the video. They will guide you through the lecture.

The Model of Christian Marriage *0:00–11:54*

- What suffuses our whole existence?

- Christians can live faithfully in any condition or society, but the gospel is also what?

- What is restored to Christian spouses in marriage?

The Problem of Marriage *11:54–24:59*

- What is the main problem in marriage that Peter wants to address?

- What should Christian women mainly want to cultivate in their lives?

After the Video

Answer the following questions after you have finished the lecture. They will help you identify and summarize the major points.

- What does the lesson mean by the *creation model* and the *redemption model*, and how are these related in this passage?

  If you are in a group, have the members discuss how they respond to these models. Ask: Do you see the goodness and grace of God in His design and restoration of marriage? Why or why not?

- How does Peter want women to act if they are married to non-Christians?

  If you are in a group, have the members consider what advice they would give to women in this situation. Ask: What would you say to them? How might you make Peter's kind and gracious concern for Christian women clear to those who may think that this passage is sexist?

- What specific commands does Peter give to husbands?

  If you are in a group, have the members discuss what they think it looks like when men honor their wives. Ask: What specific examples come to mind?

PRAYER

Commit what you have learned from God's Word in this lesson to prayer.

- Praise God for creating marriage and restoring its original goodness through the gospel.
- Confess ways that you have dishonored and failed to love your spouse.
- Thank God for His grace in the gospel, through which spouses can forgive each other and marriages can be healed.
- Ask God to bless the marriages in your church, strengthening them so that they display the gospel.

REVIEW QUIZ

Use these multiple-choice questions to measure what you learned from this lesson.

1. What verb begins both this passage and the previous passage?
   a. Love
   b. Be kind
   c. Suffer
   d. Be subject
2. What relationship should a Christian marriage mirror?
   a. A ruler and his subjects
   b. God and the temple
   c. Christ and the church
   d. A pastor and his congregation
3. According to this passage, what should a wife bring to her husband?
   a. Power
   b. Glory
   c. Wealth
   d. Wisdom
4. Where does Peter say that Christian women should look for a model of female godliness?
   a. Female preachers
   b. Their mothers
   c. Women in Scripture
   d. Christian friends
5. Peter says that a woman married to an unbelieving husband should talk about the gospel with him at every moment.
   a. True
   b. False
6. What are married women called to be for their husbands?
   a. Helpers
   b. Motivators
   c. Inspirations
   d. Subjects

Answer Key—Returning to Eden

REFLECTION & DISCUSSION QUESTIONS

Before the Video

What Do You Think?

These are personal questions. The answers should be based on your own knowledge and experience.

Scripture Reading

- How would you describe this original picture of marriage before Adam and Eve sinned? Does it have any relevance to Christian marriages today? Why or why not?

  This description of Adam and Eve suggests harmony, intimacy, and freedom. As "one flesh," they are united in a unique way. While Christians do not return to a sinless state in this life, they can experience a restoration of this original harmony in some ways. As a Christian husband and wife together submit to Christ in a desire to glorify Him, they experience something of this original design.

During the Video

The Model of Christian Marriage

- What suffuses our whole existence?

  Grace suffuses our whole existence. God's grace enables us to submit to others, and others see the grace of the gospel in us when we live as servants.

- Christians can live faithfully in any condition or society, but the gospel is also what?

  The gospel is also countercultural. We serve our employers or political leaders, but we do not belong to them. We belong to Christ. Our graciousness reveals this higher loyalty.

- What is restored to Christian spouses in marriage?

  In marriage, Christians can experience some of the original harmony and freedom of creation. Before Adam and Eve sinned, they had a union in marriage that glorified God. As Christians begin to live out the new creation through the gospel, they also live out God's original design for marriage.

The Problem of Marriage

- What is the main problem in marriage that Peter wants to address?

The main problem is Christian women's being married to non-Christian men. Peter wants wives to know how the principle of submission that he has been talking about applies to this situation, in which the husband and wife do not submit together to Christ. This relates to the general question of how to share the gospel with any non-Christian family members.

- What should Christian women mainly want to cultivate in their lives?

  Christian women should focus on cultivating Christian character. Inner beauty matters far more than outer beauty. As a general principle, focusing on one's character more than one's appearance applies as much to Christian men as Christian women.

After the Video

- What does the lesson mean by the *creation model* and the *redemption model*, and how are these related in this passage?

  Creation model *refers to God's original design for marriage, which Adam and Eve experienced before the fall.* Redemption model *refers to the new creation, the new life we have through the gospel. The New Testament draws these together in several places. The husband's gracious leadership and the wife's willing submission reflect the redemption model, in which Christians submit to the sacrificial leadership of Christ. As Christian husbands and wives together submit to Christ, they reveal the gospel to those around them.*

- How does Peter want women to act if they are married to non-Christians?

  He urges women to make the gospel attractive through their behavior. Constantly telling someone to change his beliefs can be offensive, especially if he lives with you. Acting in a way that reveals the character of Christ, however, can be attractive and lead to opportunities to share the gospel. This teaching can apply to any family or long-term relationship.

- What specific commands does Peter give to husbands?

  Peter tells husbands to live in an understanding way with their wives. He wants husbands to honor them. This requires lifelong care and attentiveness, and gratitude to God for the gift of a Christian spouse.

REVIEW QUIZ

1. **D.**

   Peter begins this passage and the previous one with the verb "be subject" (1 Peter 2:13; 3:1). This reflects his emphasis on servanthood as the mark of the Christian. Our willingness to serve in earthly vocations shows our submission to the Lord of the universe.

2. **C.**
A Christian marriage should reflect Christ and the church. The husband reflects Christ's relationship to the church as he serves and sacrifices himself for his wife. The wife then responds to this love by honoring and trusting her husband. The mutual subordination shows a picture of the gospel.

3. **B.**
A godly wife glorifies her husband. This reflects both God's original design for marriage and the new-creation reality of Christ and His church.

4. **C.**
A Christian woman might have a godly mother or friends, but Peter here instructs women to look to the godly women of Scripture as models of faithful submission.

5. **B.**
Peter instructs women to behave in a way that will make their faith attractive. Rather than forcing conversations about the gospel, they should instead act in gracious ways that may create opportunities for gospel conversations.

6. **A.**
Women may at times inspire or motivate their husbands through their love and their virtues, but Eve was created to be a helper (Gen. 2:20–22). That best characterizes how a wife should see her relationship to her husband.

8

Blessing Our Enemies

INTRODUCTION

Christians are called to be different from the world. But this difference allows us to be a blessing to the world. Our different lifestyle shows Christ to the world, especially as we respond to hostility with grace and love. In this lesson, Dr. Ferguson shows how the gospel enables us to bless not only each other but even the enemies of Christ.

LEARNING GOALS

When you have finished this lesson, you should be able to:

- Describe how communion with God and His church is necessary to the Christian life
- Explain how Christians should respond to those who oppose them
- Recognize the difference between suffering for Christ's sake and suffering as a result of sin

KEY IDEAS

- Christians depend on their church family in order to face a hostile world.
- God calls Christians to respond to opposition with blessings instead of hostility.
- When Christians bless their enemies, it opens doors to the gospel.

REFLECTION & DISCUSSION QUESTIONS

Before the Video

What Do You Think?

Take a moment to answer the following questions. They will prepare you for the lecture.

- Do you think of your church as a place that offers encouragement and strength? Why or why not?

- Can you think of a time when someone was hostile to you because of your faith? If so, how did you respond?

Scripture Reading

> *When he had washed their feet and put on his outer garments and resumed his place, he said to them, "Do you understand what I have done to you? You call me Teacher and Lord, and you are right, for so I am. If I then, your Lord and Teacher, have washed your feet, you also ought to wash one another's feet. For I have given you an example, that you also should do just as I have done to you."*
>
> —John 13:12–15

- What did Jesus do for His disciples? What does He want them to learn from His action? How could you apply this teaching to your relationships at church?

During the Video

Answer the following questions while you watch the video. They will guide you through the lecture.

How Should Christians Respond to Hostility? *0:00–13:06*

- What does the word "finally" at the beginning of this passage mean?

- What characteristic, perfectly illustrated in Jesus, should we hope to find in other Christians?

- What form of blessing for Christians does this lesson identify?

The Difference of the Christian Life *13:06–24:44*

- Nothing else matters as long as we know what?

- How may modern evangelistic techniques be in tension with this passage?

After the Video

Answer the following questions after you have finished the lecture. They will help you identify and summarize the major points.

- Why do Christians need the church to live a Christian life? How does the church help us?

  If you are in a group, have the members describe the role of their church community in their lives. Ask: Do you consistently seek to find spiritual strength in the church? Why or why not?

- Why is the world hostile to Christians? How does this knowledge help us respond to hostility in the right way?

  If you are in a group, ask the members whether they often face opposition—anger, mockery, exclusion, etc.—because of their faith and, if so, how they tend to respond. Ask about their actions and speech as well as their thoughts and emotions.

- If Christians are not different from the world, especially in their response to enemies, what are the consequences?

  If you are in a group, have the members consider whether they agree with Dr. Ferguson's description of contemporary Christianity. Ask: Do you see Christians acting in similar ways? If so, what consequences do you see?

PRAYER

Commit what you have learned from God's Word in this lesson to prayer.

- Praise God for the blessings He brings through the church.
- Confess ways that you have responded to enemies with anger or unkindness.
- Thank God for providing His people with the strength to react to hostility with grace.
- Ask God for strength as you face new temptations to live in anger and resentment toward the world.

REVIEW QUIZ

Use these multiple-choice questions to measure what you learned from this lesson.

1. What will the church enable us to be in difficult situations?
   a. Stable
   b. Powerful
   c. Sober
   d. Shrewd

2. Christians are different from the world in their actions, but they are also different from the world in what else?
   a. Vocations
   b. Politics
   c. Reactions
   d. Education

3. If Christians respond to hostility with hostility, what will they miss out on?
   a. Peace
   b. Eternal life
   c. Cultural engagement
   d. Blessing

4. What should we always be prepared to offer unbelievers?
   a. Our wisdom
   b. Our political opinions
   c. Moral correction
   d. A defense of our faith

5. Because of their sin, non-Christians can never recognize when Christians do good.
   a. True
   b. False

6. What gives us courage to face hostility by reminding us that we are safe from God's judgment?
   a. Our faithfulness
   b. Our baptism
   c. Our sense of peace
   d. Our clean conscience

Answer Key—Blessing Our Enemies

REFLECTION & DISCUSSION QUESTIONS

Before the Video

What Do You Think?

These are personal questions. The answers should be based on your own knowledge and experience.

Scripture Reading

- What did Jesus do for His disciples? What does He want them to learn from His action? How could you apply this teaching to your relationships at church?

  Jesus washed His disciples' feet. Jesus tells them that this action is an example to them. They should wash one another's feet, meaning that they should serve one another with humility.

During the Video

How Should Christians Respond to Hostility?

- What does the word "finally" at the beginning of this passage mean?

  Peter does not mean that "finally" introduces the last thing that he will talk about. Instead, the word signals a transition. It means "Now that we have dealt with this, let us move on." What comes next will build on what he has just finished talking about in the previous section.

- What characteristic, perfectly illustrated in Jesus, should we hope to find in other Christians?

  Jesus perfectly illustrated tenderheartedness. Other Christians can show us this same sacrificial love. It is a source of strength to us, and it allows us to be a source of strength to others because no one goes to someone with a hard heart in times of distress, but everyone goes to someone who has an open, sympathetic, tender heart.

- What form of blessing for Christians does this lesson identify?

  There is a blessing that comes only to those who bless when they are reviled. When we react with kindness and love toward enemies, we are drawn closer to Christ. We better understand Him, and we see that the opposition we face is about Him and not us.

The Difference of the Christian Life

- Nothing else matters as long as we know what?

  Nothing else matters as long as we know that God is with us. His Holy Spirit lives in us and sanctifies us. If we know this, no situation will seem impossible.

- How may modern evangelistic techniques be in tension with this passage?

  Many Christians in the past several decades have evangelized by approaching non-Christians and asking them questions. These questions prompt those answering to think about their ultimate beliefs and whether they are at peace with God. In this passage, though, Peter says that non-Christians will ask Christians about their faith when they see how differently Christians respond to hostility. This does not undercut the need for evangelism but calls us to live distinct lives, especially in the face of persecution.

After the Video

- Why do Christians need the church to live a Christian life? How does the church help us?

  The church encourages us. In the church, Christians find those who love them, care for them, nurture them, strengthen them, and pray for them. Christians find an identity in the fellowship of the church. All these things give Christians the stability to respond to difficulty in a way that imitates Christ.

- Why is the world hostile to Christians? How does this knowledge help us respond to hostility in the right way?

  The world is hostile to Christians because it is hostile to God, who has sent the church into the world with a mission. Knowing this, we can be comforted because we share in Christ's suffering. This knowledge also helps us respond to hostility as Christ did, suffering for the sake of righteousness and seeking to be a blessing to our enemies.

- If Christians are not different from the world, especially in their response to enemies, what are the consequences?

  If Christians act like the world, non-Christians will think that Christians are part of the world. They will have no reason to ask what we believe in or what causes us to be different. Therefore, there will be few opportunities to share the gospel. No one will think that Christians have anything unusual to offer.

REVIEW QUIZ

1. **A.**
   The church strengthens Christians in many ways, but the lesson emphasizes stability. The church helps us to be stable when we face hostility and trouble.

2. **C.**
   Christians do not necessarily differ from non-Christians in their appearance, politics, or education. Our reactions to enemies, though, mark us out as different. When we respond to hostility with gentleness and love, we reveal the distinctive character of Christ.

3. **D.**
   When we respond to hostility with hostility, we miss out on blessings. In particular, we miss the blessing of greater intimacy with Christ, who absorbed reviling and responded to enemies in love.

4. **D.**
   Christians should be prepared to make a defense of their hope in Christ. People will be more likely to ask us about our faith when our faith makes us different from the world. When asked, we need to be prepared to give an account for our hope.

5. **B.**
   In spite of their sinful nature, non-Christians can still often recognize and acknowledge the good that Christians do. Knowing this provides a strong motivation for Christians to do good, even if it leads to suffering.

6. **B.**
   Our baptism reminds us of our eternal security in Christ. Through baptism, the waters of God's judgment have already covered us, because they covered Jesus on the cross. Remembering this can strengthen us as we encounter those who are opposed to Christ and the gospel.

9

Arm Yourselves

INTRODUCTION

To follow Christ, Peter says, we must arm ourselves. But this is not a call to carry earthly weapons. Instead, we arm ourselves with a new way of thinking. The willingness to suffer for others exists only in those whose lives are not dominated by sin. In this lesson, Dr. Ferguson explains how Christians must think rightly about themselves and what Christ has done to free them from sin.

LEARNING GOALS

When you have finished this lesson, you should be able to:

- Describe how Christians must think of their relationship to sin
- Explain how Christians' lives should look to non-Christians

KEY IDEAS

- Christians are not morally perfect, but sin no longer dominates their lives.
- When non-Christians are surprised by the way Christians live, it shows the church's heavenly nature.
- Focusing on eternity will change how we live now.

REFLECTION & DISCUSSION QUESTIONS

Before the Video

What Do You Think?

Take a moment to answer the following questions. They will prepare you for the lecture.

- What do you think has more of an influence on the way you live: your thoughts or your emotions?

- Do you think about the end of the world very often? Why or why not? How might thinking about this affect your life?

Scripture Reading

Put on the whole armor of God, that you may be able to stand against the schemes of the devil. For we do not wrestle against flesh and blood, but against the rulers, against the authorities, against the cosmic powers over this present darkness, against the spiritual forces of evil in the heavenly places.

—Ephesians 6:11–12

- What kinds of enemies do Christians have? What kind of "armor" seems fitting to use against such enemies?

During the Video

Answer the following questions while you watch the video. They will guide you through the lecture.

The New Life *0:00–13:17*

- What are the two different ways that Peter wants us to think about Christ?

- In this passage, Peter is still teaching about suffering, but what is different about his focus?

The End Is Near *13:17–24:32*

- What should Christians want non-Christians to say about us?

- What future event should Christians keep in the forefront of their minds?

- What should be our motive for using our spiritual gifts?

After the Video

Answer the following questions after you have finished the lecture. They will help you identify and summarize the major points.

- What best describes the Christian's relationship to sin?

  If you are in a group, have the members discuss how they usually think about their sin. Ask: Does it feel as though sin masters you? Do you feel victorious over it? Why do you feel the way you do?

- What about the church might non-Christians find shocking?

  If you are in a group, ask the members how often they have brought non-Christians to church. Ask: Has a non-Christian visiting your church ever been surprised by what he or she saw and heard? If so, why?

- Why would thinking about our future life help us live as Christians now?

  If you are in a group, have the members share what they believe about the final judgment. Ask: How often do you think about it? Do you look forward to it in fear or in hope? Why?

PRAYER

Commit what you have learned from God's Word in this lesson to prayer.

- Praise God for saving you from the dominion of sin.
- Confess ways that you neglect to think of the things that arm you for the Christian life.
- Thank God that we can look forward to the day of judgment in hope instead of fear.
- Ask God for help remembering the truths that steady and guide you.

REVIEW QUIZ

Use these multiple-choice questions to measure what you learned from this lesson.

1. What occupation was Jesus compared to in this lesson?
    a. Lawyer
    b. Doctor
    c. Elementary-school teacher
    d. Preacher
2. To suffer like Christ, what must we have died to?
    a. The need for money
    b. The dominion of sin
    c. Physical and emotional desires
    d. The fear of God
3. What do Christians need to arm themselves with?
    a. Good works
    b. Prayer strategies
    c. Right thinking
    d. Memory verses
4. What best characterizes the sinful life that Christians have left behind?
    a. Satisfaction
    b. Freedom
    c. Futility
    d. Pain
5. If non-Christians are surprised by what they see in the church, it is an indication that something heavenly is present among God's people.
    a. True
    b. False
6. According to this lesson, what helps us focus on the future life?
    a. Our imaginations
    b. Christian love
    c. Studying prophecy
    d. Grief over our sins

Answer Key—Arm Yourselves

REFLECTION & DISCUSSION QUESTIONS

Before the Video

What Do You Think?

These are personal questions. The answers should be based on your own knowledge and experience.

Scripture Reading

- What kinds of enemies do Christians have? What kind of "armor" seems fitting to use against such enemies?

  Christians' enemies are spiritual and not human. They are "cosmic powers" and "spiritual forces of evil." Therefore, the armor of Christians must be spiritual, which the Apostle Paul describes in the rest of this passage (Eph. 6:10–17). Earthly, physical weapons will be of no help against these demonic forces that lie behind the church's human enemies.

During the Video

The New Life

- What are the two different ways that Peter wants us to think about Christ?

  Peter wants us to think about Christ as our Savior and our example. He is our Savior because He died on the cross for us, which saved us from our sins, but His example also teaches us how to live as Christians.

- In this passage, Peter is still teaching about suffering, but what is different about his focus?

  Earlier in the letter, Peter focused on the suffering that comes from persecution. Now he says that the only people willing to endure such suffering are those who have died to their old sinful way of life.

The End Is Near

- What should Christians want non-Christians to say about us?

  Christians should want unbelievers to say that the church seems like life as it was meant to be. They should be struck by its difference from the world and want to know why it is different.

- What future event should Christians keep in the forefront of their minds?

  Christians should keep their minds on the last judgment. For Christians, this is not a frightening thought. Instead, since Christ has borne our judgment on the cross, Christians think about the final judgment as the beginning of an endless future life with God.

- What should be our motive for using our spiritual gifts?

  Christians should desire to use their spiritual gifts to serve others and not mainly for personal fulfillment. For that reason, Christians should first try to identify needs in the church and try to meet them rather than focusing on a place to use their gifts.

After the Video

- What best describes the Christian's relationship to sin?

  Sanctification is a lifelong process. Christians will not be perfect until we see Christ face-to-face. But we are dead to sin as a way of life. We see its futility. We fight against it. We repent of it. Sin does not dominate our lives the way it dominates the lives of non-Christians.

- What about the church might non-Christians find shocking?

  The church can be surprising to non-Christians because Christians do not pursue the same pleasures as the world. Unbelievers cannot understand why Christians do not prize what everyone else seems to prize. It does not make sense to them. If Christians are not surprising to those outside the church, it likely means that the gospel is not having much effect on the church's way of life.

- Why would thinking about our future life help us live as Christians now?

  Thinking about eternity gives us a new motivation in life. Christians know that eternity is long and glorious, so they treat life here on earth in a fundamentally different way from those who do not share our hope. As Christians live backward from the future, they become better able to serve selflessly.

REVIEW QUIZ

1. **C.**
   Jesus was compared to an elementary-school teacher because Christians learn from His example. As we study His life, we learn what a life devoted to the gospel should look like.

2. **B.**
   To suffer for Christ, Christians need to have died to the dominion of sin. Christians know that they are free from sin's rule because Christ overthrew sin on the cross. This changes how Christians see money and their desires but does not eliminate the role of these things in the Christian life.

3. **C.**
   Good works, thoughtful prayer, and Bible memorization are all vital for Christians,

but the main point in this lesson is that right thinking orients the whole Christian life. Without understanding our relationship to God, Christ, sin, and our past lives, we are not armed as we must be. The truth of the gospel directs the Christian life.

4. **C.**
   Those still under the dominion of sin might say that they are satisfied or free, but in the end their lives are futile. They are slaves to their passions, following the trends of this world. After death, they will face judgment.

5. **A.**
   It is an encouragement to God's people when non-Christians are surprised by the church. This surprise indicates that there is something different among God's people. The Holy Spirit's presence leads to patterns of life and thought that non-Christians do not encounter anywhere else.

6. **B.**
   As Christians use their gifts to serve one another, they help one another turn away from worldly patterns of thought. They remind one another of their future resurrection when their hope will be fulfilled. This love for one another brings glory to Christ.

10

How Should Christians Suffer?

INTRODUCTION

Everyone suffers, including Christians. But as exiles in this world, Christians suffer in distinctive ways. Their suffering follows the pattern of the gospel. Peter wants his readers to understand this, so that they will be encouraged and comforted as they face trials. In this chapter, Dr. Ferguson describes the unique characteristics of suffering that Christians should expect as they seek to live faithfully.

LEARNING GOALS

When you have finished this lesson, you should be able to:

- Explain why suffering is an integral part of the Christian life
- Identify five principles that characterize Christian suffering

KEY IDEAS

- Christians should expect suffering as a natural part of the Christian life.
- Christians should suffer for the sake of Christ and not because of their own wrongdoing.
- Christians should see trials as opportunities to be faithful.

REFLECTION & DISCUSSION QUESTIONS

Before the Video

What Do You Think?

Take a moment to answer the following questions. They will prepare you for the lecture.

- In our broken world, everyone suffers. Do you see the suffering that Christians experience as unique? Why or why not?

- When you suffer, do you tend to think that something has gone wrong? Why or why not? Do you ever see trouble as an opportunity from God to grow in your faith?

Scripture Reading

Shadrach, Meshach, and Abednego answered and said to the king, "O Nebuchadnezzar, we have no need to answer you in this matter. If this be so, our God whom we serve is able to deliver us from the burning fiery furnace, and he will deliver us out of your hand, O king. But if not, be it known to you, O king, that we will not serve your gods or worship the golden image that you have set up." Then Nebuchadnezzar was filled with fury, and the expression of his face was changed against Shadrach, Meshach, and Abednego. He ordered the furnace heated seven times more than it was usually heated. And he ordered some of the mighty men of his army to bind Shadrach, Meshach, and Abednego, and to cast them into the burning fiery furnace.

—Daniel 3:16–20

- Shadrach, Meshach, and Abednego were Jewish exiles in Babylon who refused to worship the idol of Nebuchadnezzar, the Babylonian king. Based on this passage, how would you characterize their suffering? What caused it? How did they face it?

During the Video

Answer the following questions while you watch the video. They will guide you through the lecture.

The First and Second Principles of Christian Suffering *0:00–14:36*

- What is the first principle of Christian suffering?

- What is the second principle of Christian suffering?

The Third to Fifth Principles of Christian Suffering *14:36–24:16*

- What is the third principle of Christian suffering?

- What is the fourth principle of Christian suffering?

- What is the fifth principle of Christian suffering?

After the Video

Answer the following questions after you have finished the lecture. They will help you identify and summarize the major points.

- Why is suffering inevitable in the Christian life?

  If you are in a group, have the members discuss whether they struggle with the problem of evil. Ask: Do you, like many people, wonder why a just and all-powerful God allows evil? More specifically, is it often hard for you to understand why God allows Christians to suffer? If so, how have you thought through these questions in the past?

- How much should we focus on suffering?

  If you are in a group, have the members discuss whether their suffering tends to consume their thoughts. Ask: What do you think God wants you to focus on when you are in pain?

- What gives us confidence that we can endure any suffering that may come?

  If you are in a group, ask the members whether they usually feel closer to Christ or further from him when they suffer.

PRAYER

Commit what you have learned from God's Word in this lesson to prayer.

- Praise God for the comfort of knowing that your suffering is not meaningless but instead has an eternal purpose.
- Confess ways that you feel resentment toward God for allowing suffering in your life.
- Thank God that His promises give us reason to look toward future suffering with hope.
- Ask God for a growing trust and contentment in His will.

REVIEW QUIZ

Use these multiple-choice questions to measure what you learned from this lesson.

1. Which word best describes how Christians should think about their suffering?
   a. Undeserved
   b. Unsurprising
   c. Unexpected
   d. Unimaginable
2. Peter warns against suffering caused by what?
   a. Illness
   b. Poverty
   c. One's own sin
   d. Overwork
3. When we suffer as a Christian, how should we feel?
   a. Ashamed
   b. Unashamed
   c. Calm
   d. Terrified
4. As we suffer, we should not let it distract us from what?
   a. Our guilt
   b. Our strengths
   c. Our enemies
   d. Our destiny
5. We do not earn greater rewards from God for suffering well.
   a. True
   b. False
6. Suffering is an opportunity for what?
   a. Taking stock
   b. Being faithful
   c. Reframing
   d. Fighting back

Answer Key—How Should Christians Suffer?

REFLECTION & DISCUSSION QUESTIONS

Before the Video

What Do You Think?

These are personal questions. The answers should be based on your own knowledge and experience.

Scripture Reading

- Shadrach, Meshach, and Abednego were Jewish exiles in Babylon who refused to worship the idol of Nebuchadnezzar, the Babylonian king. Based on this passage, how would you characterize their suffering? What caused it? How did they face it?

  Shadrach, Meshach, and Abednego suffered for righteousness' sake. They had not sinned. Instead, they faced death because they refused to worship an idol. They were not ashamed of their suffering, but clearly explained to the king where they stood. Rather than relying on their own courage and fortitude, they placed their confidence in God's power and care. They did not assume that God would save them from the king's furnace but instead rested in His sovereign will.

During the Video

The First and Second Principles of Christian Suffering

- What is the first principle of Christian suffering?

  The first principle is that Christians should not be surprised by suffering. Christians follow Christ and trust in His cross. As they follow Him, they follow His pattern of suffering service.

- What is the second principle of Christian suffering?

  The second principle is that Christians should not be the cause of their own suffering. If they suffer as punishment for their sin, they follow the pattern of the world and not the pattern of Christ. Such suffering endangers the glory of Christ's name. Christians are blessed when they suffer for the sake of the gospel.

The Third to Fifth Principles of Christian Suffering

- What is the third principle of Christian suffering?

  The third principle is that Christians should not be ashamed of their suffering. If people oppose us because of our faith in Christ, we know that we have honor in God's sight.

- What is the fourth principle of Christian suffering?

  The fourth principle is that Christians should not be obsessed with their suffering. The final judgment is coming. Compared to this event, everything that happens in this life is small. It will all pass away. As Christians remember their assurance of eternal life through Christ, their minds can move past their suffering.

- What is the fifth principle of Christian suffering?

  The fifth principle is that Christians should see trials as opportunities to be faithful. Rather than merely enduring suffering, we should trust God and serve Him in times of trial.

After the Video

- Why is suffering inevitable in the Christian life?

  We are united to Christ. What happened to Him will happen to us. Our lives follow the pattern of the cross and the resurrection. We continually die to sin and continually grow in newness of life through the Holy Spirit. God sends trials to test our faith. As we rely on Christ in our suffering, it shows us that we can stand firm.

- How much should we focus on suffering?

  We need to know that suffering as a Christian is inevitable. We need to know that God has a purpose for our suffering. But this does not mean that we should be focused on our suffering all the time. Instead, we should put our suffering in perspective by looking to the future resurrection.

- What gives us confidence that we can endure any suffering that may come?

  The presence and promises of Christ give us confidence as we anticipate future suffering. Suffering will draw us closer to Christ, who suffered and then rose to glory. In our suffering, we remember that we are moving toward our own future glory. Christ has promised to give us the crown of righteousness and glory that He earned, and He is faithful. We know that He will sustain us no matter what.

REVIEW QUIZ

1. **B.**
   Our suffering as Christians should be unsurprising. It is an integral part of the gospel and the Christian life. Christians suffer because they follow the pattern of the cross.

2. **C.**
   Peter warns against suffering caused by Christians' own sin. This is not uniquely Christian suffering, and it is not blessed. It does not bring glory to God.

3. **B.**
   When we suffer as Christians for doing God's will, we should not feel ashamed. The

world may see our lives as shameful, but our suffering is not shameful before God. Instead, it is our honor to suffer for the sake of the gospel.

4. **D.**
   When our suffering overwhelms us, it can drown out all other realities. As we experience difficulties and pain, we should keep our minds on our future resurrection.

5. **A.**
   God will bless us as we suffer for His sake, but we do not earn rewards. Everything in the Christian life, both in the present and in eternity, is the result of God's grace toward us in the gospel.

6. **B.**
   Suffering is an opportunity for being faithful. As we suffer, we entrust ourselves to God and seek to serve Him.

11

Shepherds Who Show the Way

INTRODUCTION

Christ has appointed certain men to watch over His people. These shepherds, called elders, have a special responsibility for supporting and guiding Christ's sheep. For that reason, they have an important role in helping the church endure suffering. In this lesson, Dr. Ferguson shows how Peter saw himself as one of these shepherds and urged elders to willingly serve and suffer for Christ's sheep.

LEARNING GOALS

When you have finished this lesson, you should be able to:

- Describe the role of elders in the church
- Explain how elders help the church endure suffering

KEY IDEAS

- As those who guard and nurture God's church, elders have a special responsibility in times of trial.
- Elders should shepherd the church willingly and not for personal gain or power.
- The fruit of faithful elders will be grateful, humble congregations.

REFLECTION & DISCUSSION QUESTIONS

Before the Video

What Do You Think?

Take a moment to answer the following questions. They will prepare you for the lecture.

- What do you believe God calls elders to do?

- Are the elders in your church a source of confidence and encouragement for you? Why or why not?

Scripture Reading

When they had finished breakfast, Jesus said to Simon Peter, "Simon, son of John, do you love me more than these?" He said to him, "Yes, Lord; you know that I love you." He said to him, "Feed my lambs." He said to him a second time, "Simon, son of John, do you love me?" He said to him, "Yes, Lord; you know that I love you." He said to him, "Tend my sheep." He said to him the third time, "Simon, son of John, do you love me?" Peter was grieved because he said to him the third time, "Do you love me?" and he said to him, "Lord, you know everything; you know that I love you." Jesus said to him, "Feed my sheep."

—John 21:15–17

- What does Jesus ask Peter? What does Jesus tell Peter to do? How might the question He asks three times relate to the calling He gives to Peter?

During the Video

Answer the following questions while you watch the video. They will guide you through the lecture.

The Shepherd's Heart *0:00–11:45*

- Peter's readers know that he is an elder and an eyewitness of the sufferings of Christ, but what else do they know about him?

- What are the two examples of shepherds that these readers can look to?

- What are the first two qualifications for elders in 1 Peter?

Shepherds as Models *11:45–24:59*

- What is the third qualification for elders in 1 Peter?

- What virtue mentioned in this passage should elders model for their congregations?

After the Video

Answer the following questions after you have finished the lecture. They will help you identify and summarize the major points.

- In this letter that focuses on Christian suffering and persecution, why does Peter take time to address elders?

  If you are in a group, have the members discuss whether they have found comfort and guidance from elders in their churches during difficult times. Ask: Have any elders modeled faithful suffering?

- What are some encouragements for elders, and why does Peter mention them?

  If you are in a group, have the members discuss whether it encourages them to think that they are the crown and joy of their elders. Ask: Do you sense that this is true? How might this affect your relationship with your elders and how you pray for your elders?

- What is the fruit of faithful eldership?

  If you are in a group, have the members discuss how the character of the elders in their churches affects the character of the congregation. Ask: Do you see humility nurtured through the example of your elders?

PRAYER

Commit what you have learned from God's Word in this lesson to prayer.

- Praise God for Jesus, the Great Shepherd, who perfectly guards His flock.
- Confess ways that you have been overly critical and unsupportive of your elders.
- Thank God for faithful elders, especially those who have watched over you.
- Ask God to strengthen the elders in His church and raise up more faithful shepherds around the world.

REVIEW QUIZ

Use these multiple-choice questions to measure what you learned from this lesson.

1. What are elders best described as?
   a. Managers
   b. Priests
   c. Coaches
   d. Shepherds
2. Who acted as an elder for Peter?
   a. Paul
   b. John the Baptist
   c. Jesus
   d. James
3. Which of the following should be the main motivation of elders?
   a. A sense of duty
   b. Loyalty to the church
   c. Heavenly rewards
   d. Love for God's people
4. Which of the following disqualifies someone for eldership?
   a. Singleness
   b. Sin
   c. Weakness
   d. Misuse of power
5. Which of the following words does *not* describe the crown that faithful elders receive?
   a. Merited
   b. Glorious
   c. Unfading
   d. Gracious
6. Which word best describes the kind of response that younger Christians will have to faithful elders?
   a. Prompt
   b. Unquestioning
   c. Dutiful
   d. Glad

Answer Key—Shepherds Who Show the Way

REFLECTION & DISCUSSION QUESTIONS

Before the Video

What Do You Think?

These are personal questions. The answers should be based on your own knowledge and experience.

Scripture Reading

- What does Jesus ask Peter? What does Jesus tell Peter to do? How might the question He asks three times relate to the calling He gives to Peter?

  Jesus asks Peter whether he loves Him. Then He calls Peter to feed His sheep: to be an elder. Jesus did this three times to restore Peter after his threefold denial. It is clear that Peter's love for Jesus means that he has the heart to care for those whom Jesus loves.

During the Video

The Shepherd's Heart

- Peter's readers know that he is an elder and an eyewitness of the sufferings of Christ, but what else do they know about him?

  Peter's readers know that he has failed. He needed to be shepherded and restored by Jesus. Therefore, he speaks not from a lofty height of moral perfection but instead from humility. His readers can relate to him.

- What are the two examples of shepherds that these readers can look to?

  Peter needed to be shepherded by Jesus, "the chief Shepherd" (1 Peter 5:4). Peter offers, therefore, the example of the perfect, sinless Shepherd, Jesus, and his own imperfect example.

- What are the first two qualifications for elders in 1 Peter?

  Elders must be motivated by a sincere love for God's people. This means, first, that they should serve willingly. They must desire to serve and care for the sheep and not assume leadership only from a sense of obligation. Second, they must not serve for their own gain. They should not become elders hoping for financial rewards or an enhancement of their reputations.

Shepherds as Models

- What is the third qualification for elders in 1 Peter?

Elders must not be domineering or intimidating. They should not serve out of love of power. Elders are called to serve the sheep and not abuse them.

- What virtue mentioned in this passage should elders model for their congregations?

  Peter calls all his readers, both elders and those who follow them, to humility. Rather than dominating the flock, elders must be humble, providing God's people with an example of submission.

After the Video

- In this letter that focuses on Christian suffering and persecution, why does Peter take time to address elders?

  Elders' leadership of the church can be especially important in times of persecution. The elders are often the first people targeted by the church's enemies, so they need to be prepared. They need to be motivated by love so that they can follow the model of Jesus, "the chief Shepherd," who laid down His life for the sheep. As they serve faithfully, elders will be models to the church of how to suffer for Christ.

- What are some encouragements for elders, and why does Peter mention them?

  Elders should be encouraged by "the unfading crown of glory" (1 Peter 5:4) that they will receive for their faithful service. The grace that God has worked in them and through them in the church will last for eternity. This crown may refer to the Christians that elders have shepherded (Phil. 4:1). Elders can endure through great difficulties, knowing how glorious the results of their labors will be.

- What is the fruit of faithful eldership?

  The fruit of faithful eldership will be a glad response from younger Christians and the whole congregation. Humble and loving eldership will lead to trust and a desire to imitate the elders' way of life. Elders characterized by loving servanthood will find that those they lead will grow to reflect that humility and willingly submit to Christ.

REVIEW QUIZ

1. **D.**
   Elders have certain managerial responsibilities, but they are described as shepherds. They guard and nurture God's people. They care for Christians' souls and guide them to Christ, the chief Shepherd. Elders, however, are not priests. They are not mediators between God and His people. Instead, they bring people to the Mediator, who is Christ.

2. **C.**
   Jesus, whom Peter calls "the chief Shepherd" (1 Peter 5:4), acted as an elder for Peter. After Peter's failures, Jesus restored him and then called him to shepherd the church as Jesus had been Shepherd to him (John 21:15–17).

3. **D.**
Peter says that the elders must shepherd "not under compulsion, but willingly" (1 Peter 5:2). When persecution comes, elders will likely be the first target. Only love for the sheep will make them fit for their responsibilities and willing, if necessary, to lay down their lives for the sheep.

4. **D.**
Certain sins and weaknesses disqualify men from eldership, but all elders remain sinners in this life. Like all of God's people, they remain dependent on God's grace every day. Misuse of power, however, is a disqualification. Elders are called to be servants.

5. **A.**
The crown of victory that brings encouragement to elders is an "unfading crown of glory" (1 Peter 5:4). Like every other good thing that Christians receive, it is a gift of God's grace. This crown recognizes elders' faithful service, but all their efforts and any success result from God's grace in their lives.

6. **D.**
This lesson mainly characterizes the response of younger Christians to faithful elders as "glad." As elders shepherd willingly and humbly, out of love for the sheep, Christians submit themselves more willingly or gladly to the elders' leadership.

12

Bound for Glory

INTRODUCTION

Throughout this letter, Peter has offered counsel to churches enduring suffering. They are sojourners and exiles in a pagan society, and this had led to trials. Now, he reminds them that behind everything is an enemy that wants to destroy them. But God's purpose for them, as it was for Jesus, is to bring them into glory. In this final lesson, Dr. Ferguson explains how only a true view of God enables us to entrust ourselves to Him, which is how we reach the glory that He has prepared for us.

LEARNING GOALS

When you have finished this lesson, you should be able to:

- Identify the church's true enemy, his intentions, and his strategies
- Explain how a true understanding of God, from His Word, protects Christians from this enemy

KEY IDEAS

- The true enemy of the church is Satan and not human rulers or societies.
- The ability to withstand our enemies comes from a true understanding of God.
- The church must watch for Satan's three main ways of attacking the church.

REFLECTION & DISCUSSION QUESTIONS

Before the Video

What Do You Think?

Take a moment to answer the following questions. They will prepare you for the lecture.

- Do you think of yourself as having enemies? If so, who comes first to mind? How do these enemies try to harm you?

- How important do you think correct theology is to the Christian life? Why?

Scripture Reading

"Simon, Simon, behold, Satan demanded to have you, that he might sift you like wheat, but I have prayed for you that your faith may not fail. And when you have turned again, strengthen your brothers." Peter said to him, "Lord, I am ready to go with you both to prison and to death." Jesus said, "I tell you, Peter, the rooster will not crow this day, until you deny three times that you know me."

—Luke 22:31–34

- What does Jesus tell Peter that Satan wants to do? What does Jesus say that He will do? What does Jesus say that Peter will do?

During the Video

Answer the following questions while you watch the video. They will guide you through the lecture.

Who Is Our Enemy? *0:00–11:19*

- What are the consequences if we do not have a right view of God?

- Why did Satan attack Peter?

Satan's Tactics *11:19–24:44*

- What are Satan's three main tactics against the church?

- When we know Satan's tactics, what can we do?

- What can God do with our failures?

After the Video

Answer the following questions after you have finished the lecture. They will help you identify and summarize the major points.

- When there is trouble in the church, where do we often focus? What might be a better way of assessing trouble in the church?

  If you are in a group, have the members discuss whether they have seen much trouble in their churches. Ask: How has the church addressed the role of Satan in these problems? To what extent should we see evil spiritual powers rather than people as the cause of trouble in the church?

- What does it mean to be sober-minded?

  If you are in a group, ask the members whether they think sober-mindedness characterizes themselves and their churches. If not, what problems has this contributed to?

- How does Peter's life demonstrate the grace of God?

  If you are in a group, ask the members whether the example of Peter's life encourages them and why.

PRAYER

Commit what you have learned from God's Word in this lesson to prayer.

- Praise God for His glorious plan for our trials.
- Confess ways that you hold on to your anxiety out of a mistrust of God.
- Thank God for carrying our anxieties as we cast them on Him.
- Ask God to help you and your church think clearly about God and be watchful for Satan's attacks.

REVIEW QUIZ

Use these multiple-choice questions to measure what you learned from this lesson.

1. What stands behind the opposition that Christians face?
   a. Secularism
   b. Pagan rulers
   c. Heresy
   d. Satan

2. To be sober-minded, we need mainly to avoid a false view of what?
   a. Society
   b. Satan
   c. God
   d. History

3. To protect the church, what should Christians first seek to recognize?
   a. The work of Satan
   b. The supernatural gifts of the Spirit
   c. The political enemies of the church
   d. The guilt of church members

4. Which of these is *not* one of Satan's main tactics against the church?
   a. Division
   b. Depression
   c. False ambition
   d. Persecution

5. If we recognize Satan's tactics, we can resist them.
   a. True
   b. False

6. God does some of His best work in us when we do what?
   a. Stand firm
   b. Stay pure
   c. Teach
   d. Fail

Answer Key—Bound for Glory

REFLECTION & DISCUSSION QUESTIONS

Before the Video

What Do You Think?

These are personal questions. The answers should be based on your own knowledge and experience.

Scripture Reading

- What does Jesus tell Peter that Satan wants to do? What does Jesus say that He will do? What does Jesus say that Peter will do?

  Jesus tells Peter that Satan wants to test or "sift" him. Then Jesus says that He will pray for Peter. In spite of Peter's protests, Jesus tells Peter that he will deny Jesus. After this, though, Peter will be restored and serve the church. Jesus tells Peter, "Strengthen your brothers."

During the Video

Who Is Our Enemy?

- What are the consequences if we do not have a right view of God?

  If we do not have a right view of God, we will become confused and vulnerable. We will be unable to entrust ourselves and our troubles to Him.

- Why did Satan attack Peter?

  Since Satan could not destroy Jesus, the builder of the church, he attacked Peter. As an Apostle, Peter was one of the major stones in God's temple, the church.

Satan's Tactics

- What are Satan's three main tactics against the church?

  Satan's three main tactics against the church are persecution, false ambition, and division. Persecution is physical intimidation that comes from the world. False ambition and division both occur within the church.

- When we know Satan's tactics, what can we do?

  If we know Satan's tactics, we can recognize his work and resist him. We resist him not by devising strategies of spiritual warfare but instead by entrusting all our troubles to God.

- What can God do with our failures?

  God can transform our failures into gifts that serve the church. We often understand God's grace most profoundly in the areas where we have failed, and this experience of grace makes us a blessing to others.

After the Video

- When there is trouble in the church, where do we often focus? What might be a better way of assessing trouble in the church?

  When there is trouble in the church, we often focus on the human causes. In the big picture, though, Satan is the church's enemy and behind all the trouble the church faces, whether from within or from without. By recognizing that we have a supernatural enemy, we can go to our source of divine strength, God, rather than mistakenly thinking that the battle is on only a human level.

- What does it mean to be sober-minded?

  Being sober-minded means having a right understanding of God and keeping this before us. True knowledge of God keeps us from confusion and spiritual drunkenness. It keeps us focused on our true source of strength: God and His grace. Only a right understanding of God will keep us steady and give us discernment about Satan and his tactics.

- How does Peter's life demonstrate the grace of God?

  Peter tells these churches that God will "restore, confirm, strengthen, and establish" them (1 Peter 5:10). This pattern reflects the work of God's grace in Peter's life. After Peter's failures, Jesus shepherded him. First, Jesus restored Peter's peace with God through the gospel. Then Jesus confirmed Peter in his ministry. Next, Jesus strengthened Peter through the power of the Holy Spirit. Finally, Jesus established him, making him able to minister to others. Peter did not earn any of this. It was all the work of God's grace.

REVIEW QUIZ

1. **D.**
   Heresy in the church, pagan political leaders, and worldly ideologies can create trouble for Christians, but Satan stands behind them all. He orchestrates everything in the world that opposes God and His people.

2. **C.**
   Being sober-minded means primarily having a right view of God. We cannot trust Him if we do not know what He is like. If we cannot trust Him, we cannot give our troubles and anxieties into His care. A true knowledge of God will also help us have an accurate view of Satan and society, but understanding God is the essential foundation.

3. **A.**
   Satan successfully attacks the church, in part, because the church tends to be oblivious to his presence and tactics. Awareness of Satan's work does not mean that the church should not recognize human sin and the reality of human enemies, but human causes are not the ultimate source of trouble in the church.

4. **B.**
   Depression can be a serious problem for many Christians, but that is not one of the main tactics mentioned in the lesson. Satan works mainly through persecution from outside the church, false ambition within the church, and division in the church over matters of secondary importance.

5. **A.**
   Peter tells his readers about Satan's tactics so that they can resist him. The church resists Satan not with human strength but through the Holy Spirit as Christians trust God and His gospel promises.

6. **D.**
   Our sin is never pleasing to God, but sometimes God does His best work in us when we fail. In His providence, He can transform those failures into gifts through which we serve others. We see this in Peter, who denied Jesus and the gospel multiple times. Through these failures, God made Peter a wise and compassionate shepherd of the church.